Table of Content

CHAPTER 1: INTRODUCTION

The intention of this project is to increase an internet crime report and managing process which is without difficulty obtainable to the public. The police division and the executive division .This process reported the complaint from indivisual through on-line and it's going to also useful to police department in catching criminals, in procedure and character may give any complaint at any time.

1.1 Background

IT Asset supervisor application solutions is an IT solution provider for a dynamic atmosphere the place trade and science procedures converge. Their strategy specializes in new methods of business combining IT innovation and adoption whilst additionally leveraging an institution's present IT assets. Their work with giant world organisations and new merchandise or services and to put into effect prudent industry and science tactics in in these days's environment.

1.2 Objectives

The undertaking is identified by using the merits of the system furnished to the person. The merits of this task are as follows: -

1 It's an online-enabled project.

2 This assignment presents consumer to enter the info via simple and interactive varieties. This is very useful for the purchaser to enter the preferred know-how through so much simplicity.

1   The purchaser is most normally extra worried related to the validity of the knowledge, whatever he's getting into. There are checks on each phases of any new construction, abilities entry or updation so that the character are not able to enter the invalid competencies, so that you could create problems at later date.

2   Fourregularly the user finds in the later levels of making use of challenge that he wants to replace one of the vital information that he entered previous. There are alternatives for him during which he can replace the records. Moreover there may be

limit for his that he can't exchange the fundamental data subject. This keeps the validity of the information to longer extent.

5 consumer is offered the option of monitoring the records he entered previous. He can see the preferred files with the kind of choices offered by using him.

6 From every a part of the challenge the user is provided with the hyperlinks through framing in order that he can go from one alternative of the undertaking to different as per the requirement. That is certain to be simple and really friendly as per the consumer is involved. That's, we will sat that the mission is user pleasant which is likely one of the principal concerns of any good undertaking.

7 information storage and retrieval will turn out to be faster and easier to keep because data is stored in a scientific manner and in a single database.

Eight determination making approach can be commonly enhanced when you consider that of turbo processing of understanding considering information collection from understanding available on laptop takes a lot less time then manual procedure.

9 Allocating of pattern outcome becomes a lot turbo since at a time the person can see the files of last years.

10 easier and turbo knowledge switch by means of present day technology associated with the laptop and conversation.

11 by means of these elements it is going to increase the efficiency, accuracy and transparency,

1.3 Purpose , Scope and Applicability

1.3.1 Purpose

The purpose of this project is to support an internet established crime document and managing technique which is with ease to be had to most of the people. The police division and the executive division.

This system registers the complaints from men and women by means of online and it's going to also precious to police division in catching criminals, in method and man or woman may give any complaint at any tie

Most commonly men and women in India are afraid to offer a grievance in police station seeing that they are full of a false worry in regards to the police department. An online grievance registration procedure will clear up the fear of the public and which also helps police division catching criminals and taking proper action.

- It is an online way to show the records.
- To overcome this issue the people Evaluation System is implemented to keep the record.
- The people can easily access the browser and give information to criminal.
- It is an online way to reporet and display the records.
- It reduces effort for people will decresese.

1.3.2 Scope

An online-established answer could also be very necessary as the solution is inherently distributive. This distributive characteristic of the net solution helps in getting the one-of-a-kind police stations to share know-how and get in touch with one yet another. Bird asked about their top issues for their nation, americans have always rated crime as a gigantic situation. Anybody who has been a sufferer of even a minor crime can attest to the affect it has on his or her life, both emotionally and in phrases of time and inconvenience coping with the aftermath. To lessen crime and the influence it has on contributors and society, criminologists must be equipped to measure and understand it. Without an equipped means of recording expertise about crimes that have came about, law enforcement agencies do not need the advantage of social science research in identifying who is prone to be victimized so they can provide safeguard, who is likely to grow to be an culprit so they are able to provide choices, and where crime is undoubtedly to arise so they can broaden patrol.

1.3.3 Applicability

Most commonly men and women in India are afraid to offer a grievance in police station seeing that they are full of a false worry in regards to the police department. An online grievance registration procedure will clear up the fear of the public and which also helps police division catching criminals and taking proper action.

Simple crime reporting is easy to install and administer.

The user interface is more intuitive.

It is able to import and use static webpage in the crime reporting

Easily create editable regions for clients within the front-end of the website.

It points effortless menu page construction and a best WYSIWYG editor, which permits handy content material formatting, snapshot importing and picture resizing.

It also gives the potential so as to add a brand new stylesheet or modify the prevailing ones.

The workflow will simplest allow the newly created web page to be noticeable to the customers when the administrator approves and publishes it.

The audit path document displays the expertise regarding all alterations made to the website pages and as a consequence helps in deterring fraud by keeping a document of which pages have been modified or deleted.

METHODOLOGY: -

The model that is essentially actuality followed is the WATER FALL MODEL, which states that the phases are prepared in a linear order. First of all the option education is done. Once that part is over the state study and project development begins. If system exists one and change and calculation of new module is needed, study of present system can be used as basic model. The design starts after the condition scrutiny is whole and the coding begins after the design is complete. Once the program design is finished, the testing is ready. In this model the classification of actions executed in a software evolution project are: -

1. Requirement Analysis
2. Project Planning
3. System design
4. Detail design Coding
5. Unit testing
6. System amalgamation & testing.

Here the linear get-collectively of these routine is critical. End of the phase and the output of one segment is the input of alternative segment. The output of each and every segment is to be constant with the overall of the method. Some of the traits of spiral mannequin are additionally incorporated like after the folks worried with the project assessment completion of every of the segment the work executed.

WATER FALL model was once being selected since all supplies had been known before and the fair of our program development is the mechanization/mechanization of an already contemporary handbook working process.

Fig 2.2: Water Fall Model

1.4 Achievements

* The process is in the end reaches at the finish line and in a position to make use of the application.

* It'll end up more worthy within the education subject.

* it's a newly noticeable schooling process.

* where it may be not work as student evaluation procedure but additionally normal cause approach.

* The system is online program so it can not be has an information loss.

* The system is partially accomplished on the grounds that it is able to use and except it's going to go all the every institutes and they will get benefit then it's going to be real success.

1.5 Oganisation of Report

Introduction: - on this phase we have already covered all aspects and facets. Now the leisure are given briefly.

•SURVEY OF science: -

In this chapter we will be discussing about the technologies on the way to be utilized in constructing our internet site.
We will be able to be comparing different related technologies that could use as an alternative.

•REQUIREMENT ANALYSIS: -

we can be defining the problem announcement of assignment. We will additionally mentioning the condition cessities.
Planning and scheduling of the mission might be outlined. Milestones of the assignment may also be defined.

We will additionally incorporate the conceptual items reminiscent of knowledge flow diagram, ER diagram, recreation diagram, Sequence diagram etc.

•METHOD DESIGN: -

On our internet site we're additionally including various common units, data Design, Schema Design, knowledge Integrity and constraints, Procedural design, good judgment Diagrams, Algorithms Design, person Interface design, safety disorders, experiment circumstances design.

CONCLUSION: -

It has been a great pleasure for me to work on this exciting and motivating project. This project proven good for me as it providing practical information of not only programming in ASP.NET and C#.NET web based presentation and no some extent Windows Application and SQL Server, but also about all action procedure related with **"Online Crime reporting".** It also provides information about the latest expertise used in emergent web permissible application and client server equipment that will be great request in future. This will provide better events and direction in future in developing projects self-reliantly.

CHAPTER 2: SURVEY OF TECHNOLOGIES

CLIENT SIDE TECHNOLOIES: -

Windows 7 or

high Browser

ASP.NET

C#.NET.

SQL SERVER

DATABASE: -

SERVER SIDE TECHNOLOGIES: -

MY SQL

SUMMARY OF TECHNOLOGIES: -

The .Internet Framework is a new multiplying platform that shortens application development in the incredibly disbursed environment of the web. The .Internet Framework is designed to meet the subsequent ambitions:

• To furnish a comfy object-oriented programming environment whether or not or no longer or no longer object code is saved and applied within the neighborhood,performed in the community but web-allotted, or performed remotely.

•   To furnish a code-execution surroundings that reduces utility deployment and versioning encounters.

• To furnish a code-execution atmosphere that assurances nontoxic execution of code, together with code created through an unknown or semi-relied on 1/3 occasion. • To furnish a code-execution atmosphere that removes the performance issues of scripted or construed environments.

• To make the developer knowledge riskless across commonly varying varieties of applications, such as home windows-established functions and internet-founded purposes.

FEATURES OF THE COMMON LANGUAGE RUNTIME

The expected language runtime manages memory, thread execution, code implementation, prcode security confirmation, compiling, and other procedure donations. These aspects are essential to the managed code that runs on the customary language runtime.

In terms of safety, managed add-ons are awarded various levels of believe, relying on a number of causes that comprise their beginning (such because the web, organization community, or nearby laptop). Which means that a managed aspect would or might not be ready to participate in file-entry operations, registry-entry operations, or different sensitive services, even supposing it is getting used in the same lively application.

The runtime enforces code entry protection. For instance, customers can believe that an executable embedded in an online web page can play an animation on disclose or sing a tune, nonetheless can not access their individual information, file method, or neighborhood. The security aspects of the runtime hence allow legit internet-deployed application to be exceptionally providing wealthy.

The runtime moreover enforces code robustness by way of utilizing imposing a strict form- and code-verification infrastructure referred to as the ordinary Form system (CTS). The CTS ensures that every one managed code is self-describing. The quite a lot of Microsoft and nil.33-celebration language compilers Generate managed code that conforms to the CTS. Due to the fact that of this that managed code can consume specific managed varieties and occasions, whilst strictly imposing kind fidelity and type protection.

Additionally, the managed surroundings of the runtime eliminates many common software issues. For illustration, the runtime often handles object design and manages references to objects, releasing them when they're no longer getting used. This computerized reminiscence administration resolves the 2 most average utility blunders, memory leaks and invalid reminiscence references.

The runtime additionally accelerates developer productiveness. For illustration, programmers can write aspects of their progress language of substitute, but take full expertise of the runtime, the class library, and add-ons written in first-class languages by the use of targeted builders. Any compiler vendor who chooses to intention the runtime can accomplish that. Language compilers that intention the .Web Framework make the points of the .Internet Framework available to reward code written in that language, extra in most cases than not easing the migration system for reward purposes.Whilst as the runtime is designed for the application of the longer term, it furthermore helps application of in at the moment and yesterday. Interoperability between managed and unmanaged code permits builders to proceed to use principal COM add-ons and DLLs.

The runtime is designed to develop efficiency. Nonetheless that the lengthy centered language runtime offers many common runtime choices, managed code just is not ever interpreted. A attribute known as just-in-time (JIT) compiling makes it possible for all managed code to run inside the native computing device language of the system on which it is executing. Meanwhile, the memory supervisor removes the chances of fragmented memory and raises reminiscence locality-of-reference to further increase efficiency.

Ultimately, the runtime can be hosted by way of immoderate-effectivity, server part purposes, paying homage to Microsoft® SQL Server™ and web figuring out offerings (IIS). This infrastructure makes it viable for you to make use of managed code to jot down down your organization simply proper judgment, at the same time however having pleasurable with one of the vital imperative satisfactory efficiency of the enterprise's first-class manufacturer servers that support runtime internet site hosting.

CLIENT APPLICATION DEVELOPMENT

Consumer functions are the neighboring to a typical form of application in residence windows-headquartered programming. These are the forms of functions that display residence windows or sorts on the laptop, enabling a client to participate in a task. Customer applications comprise purposes comparable to phrase processors and spreadsheets, as good as personalized trade applications much like talents-entry devices, reporting tools, and many others. Purchaser purposes most often appoint home windows, menus, buttons, and different GUI reasons, they probably seemingly access neighborhood assets such because the file process and peripherals corresponding to printers.

Yet one more type of buyer utility is the customary ActiveX manipulate (now changed via the managed house residence home windows types manipulate) deployed over the online. This program could also be very like amazing consumer purposes: it's accomplished natively, has entry to nearby belongings, and includes graphical factors.

Previously, builders created such purposes utilizing C/C++ along with the Microsoft groundwork publications (MFC) or with a rapid utility development (RAD) environment paying homage to Microsoft® noticeable common®. The .Internet Framework incorporates factors of those present products right into a single, constant progress environment that broadly simplifies the development of patron functions.

The windows forms courses contained inside the .. Which that you would be able to effectively create command home windows, buttons, menus, toolbars, and different reveal factors with the flexibility valuable to accommodate relocating enterprise needs.

For illustration, the .Net Framework offerings easy properties to keep an eye on image qualities related to forms. In some cases the underlying strolling procedure does now not aid altering these facets immediately, and in these situations the .Web Framework robotically recreates the types. This is one between many methods where the .Web Framework integrates the developer boundary, making coding easier and more regular.

Not like ActiveX panels, dwelling windows types controls have semi-relied on access to a person's computer. This means that binary or natively executing code can entry some of the belongings on the individual's system (comparable to GUI explanations and constrained file entry) with out being ready to access or compromise different property. Due to the fact that of code entry protection, many features that after desired to be hooked up on a consumer's procedure can now be safely set up by way of the online. Your functions can put in force the elements of a area utility even as being positioned like a web based web page.

SQL SERVER TABLES

SQL Server stores records linking to each other in a table. Dissimilar tables are shaped for the various groups of information. Related tables are grouped collected to form a database.

PRIMARY KEY

Each table in SQL Server has a subject or a combo of fields that exclusively categorizes each record within the desk. The certain identifier is called the predominant Key, or excellently the significant thing. The important key supplies the method to differentiate one file from all different in a table. It papers the person and the database tactic to identify, find and refer to 1 exclusive report in the database.

RELATIONAL DATABASE

typically all of the evidence of curiosity to a trade operation can also be stored in one desk. SQL Server makes it very handy to hyperlink the information in more than one tables. Corresponding an worker to the sector where they work is one illustration. That is what makes SQL Server a interactive database management system, or RDBMS. It retailers information in two or extra tables and allows for you to outline family members between the desk and permits you to define relations between the tables.

FOREIGN KEY

When a area is one desk races the foremost key of additional discipline is known as a international key. A overseas secret's a subject or a bunch of fields in a single table whose values in shape those of the main key of another table.

REFERENTIAL INTEGRITY

Not best does SQL Server permit you to link more than a few tables, it also conserves consistency between them. Guaranteeing that the info amongst associated tables is thoroughly matched is denoted to as conserving referential integrity.

DATA ABSTRACTION

A most important cause of a database method is to furnish users with an abstract view of the info. This scheme hides designated details of how the information is saved and stored. Data idea is divided into three phases.

Physical level: this is the lowermost level of abstraction at which one defines how the information are truely saved.

Conceptual Level: At this level of database notion all the attributed and what data are actually stored is termed and entries and liaison among them.

View level: This is the uppermost level of concept at which one describes only part of the database.

ADVANTAGES OF RDBMS

Dismissal can be avoided

Irregularity can be eliminated

Data can be Shared

Principles can be enforced

Safekeeping restrictions ca be applied

Integrity can be sustained

Differing requirements can be balanced

Data objectivity can be achieved.

DISADVANTAGES OF DBMS

A giant disadvantage of the DBMS method is fee. In addition to the price of purchasing of constructing the program, the hardware needs to be upgraded to permit for the extensive packages and the workspace required For his or her execution and storage.

Whilst centralization reduces duplication, the dearth of duplication requires that the database be thoroughly backed up in order that in case of failure the data can be recovered.

FEATURES OF SQL SERVER (RDBMS)

SQL SERVER is among the main database management programs (DBMS) seeing that it is probably the most real Database that meets the inflexible requisites of at gift's most demanding know-how packages. From worrying resolution support packages (DSS) to often basically the most rigorous online transaction processing (OLTP) utility, even software that require simultaneous DSS and OLTP access to the equal prime expertise, SQL Server leads the enterprise in each effectivity and capability

SQL SERVER is a truly moveable, distributed.SQL SERVER RDBMS is high competence fault tolerant DBMS which is expressly considered for on-line businesses processing and for production with significant database value.

SQL SERVER with contacts processing alternative offers two facets which make a contribution to very excessive stage of transaction processing amount, which might be

PORTABILITY

SQL SERVER is wholly moveable to greater than eighty targeted hardware and working techniques platforms, together with UNIX, MSDOS, OS/2, Macintosh and dozens of proprietary stages. This portability offers whole independence to pick the database sever platform that encounters the process necessities.

OPEN SYSTEMS

SQL SERVER presents a leading employment of company –regular SQL. SQL Server's open constitution integrates SQL SERVER and non –SQL SERVER DBMS with industries most whole assortment of instruments, utility, and 1/3 get together program merchandise SQL Server's Open constitution presents obvious entry to expertise from other relational database and even non-relational database.

DISTRIBUTED DATA SHARING

SQL Server's networking and disbursed database capabilities to contact information saved on far flung server with the equal ease as if the proof was once saved on a single regional computer. A single SQL declaration can access information at many websites. Which you can retailer knowledge the place system necessities akin to activities, protection or availability directive.

SOPHISTICATED CONCURRENCY CONTROL

Real World applications demand access to critical information. With most database systems application becomes "competition certain" – which performance is restrained no longer By way of the CPU vigour or via disk I/O, but procurer competent on one a different for potential entry . SQL Server employments full, unrestricted row-degree bolting and contributors free queries to lower and in many occurrences completely eliminates struggle wait occasions.

NO I/O BOTTLENECKS

SQL Server commits contacts with at most sequential log file on disk at commit time, On excessive throughput techniques, one sequential writes normally team commit more than one transactions. Data read with the aid of the transaction remains as shared memory so that different transactions may just entry that knowledge without studying it again from disk. On account that fast commits write all knowledge fundamental to the healing to the log file, modified blocks are written again to the database independently of the transaction commit, when written from reminiscence to disk.

CHAPTER 3: REQUIREMENTS AND ANALYSIS

3.1 Problem Definition

The software, Site Pioneer is planned for management of web sites from a isolated location.

INTRODUCTION

Purpose: The most important intent for concocting this record is to provide a over-all insight into the analysis and specifications of the present process or drawback and for influential the operating appearances of the method.

Scope: This Document plays a vigorous role in the development life cycle (SDLC) and it defines the complete situation of the system. It is destined for use by the developers and will be the basic during testing phase. Any changes made to the supplies in the future will have to go through formal change approval procedure.

3.2 Requirements Specification

OUTPUT DESIGN

Outputs from pc methods are required principally to keep in touch the outcome of processing to customers. They are additionally used to furnish a everlasting replica of the outcome for later session. The more than a few varieties of outputs most often are:

1 outside Outputs, whose trip spot is outside the tuition,.

2 inside Outputs whose vacation spot is with in institution and they're the Three consumer's foremost interface with the computer.Four Operational outputs whose use is most effective with inside the laptop division.

3   Interface outputs, which incorporate the person in communicating straight with

Output Media:

In the subsequent stage it's to be decided that which medium is the most appropriate for the output. The fundamental issues when determining about the output media are:

1 The suitability for the gadget to the specified software.

2 the necessity for a difficult copy.

3 The response time required.

4 The location of the customers

5 The application and hardware on hand.

Preserving in view the above description the project is to have outputs as a rule coming underneath the class of interior outputs.

INPUT. DESIGN

. The principal objective for the duration of the input design is as given below:

• To provide a fee-mighty approach of enter.

• To achive the very best conceivable stage of accuracy.

• To brand sure that the enter is suitable and unspoken via the user.

INPUT TYPES:

It is essential to control the various types of inputs. Inputs can be branded as follows:

External contributions, which are prime efforts for the system.
Internal contributions, which are user communications with the system.

INPUT MEDIA:

At this stage choice has to be made about the input media. To assemble about the input media devotion has to be given to;

Type of input

Flexibility of format

Speediness

Accuracy

Authentication methods

Refusal rates

Ease of improvement

    Storage and handling

    supplies Safekeeping

Easy to use

Lightness

Preserving in view the above description of the input types and input media, it is usually stated that most of the inputs are of the type of interior and interactive. As

enter information is to be the immediately keyed in by way of the person, the keyboard can be viewed to be nearly the most suitable enter gadget.

ERROR AVOIDANCE

At this phase care is to be taken to warrant that input data leftovers truthful form the phase at which it is recorded upto the stage in which the data is imaginary by the system. This can be accomplished only by earnings of alert controller each time the data is handled.

ERROR DETECTION

Even though every strength is make to avoid the amount of errors, still a small amount of errors is always likely to occur, these types of errors can be exposed by using proofs to check the input data.

DATA VALIDATION

Systems are designed to notice blunders in data at a slash level of detail. Data validations were integrated within the approach in nearly each correction where there is a possibility for the person to commit blunders. Validations have been combined where necessary.

The approach is intended to be a person friendly one. In other words the system has been designed to be in contact with no trouble with the consumer. The method has been designed with pop up menus.

USER INTERFACE DESIGN

It is important to consult the system users and debate their needs while designing the user interface:

USER INTERFACE SYSTEMS CAN BE BROADLY CLASIFIED AS:

1. User initiated interface the user is in charge, controlling the progress of the user/mainframe discussion. In the computer-initiated interface, the computer chooses the next sta interaction.

2. **Computer initiated interfaces**

In the pc initiated interfaces the computer guides the development of the consumer/desktop speak. Information is displayed and the client response of the computing device takes motion or suggests additional working out.

USER_INITIATED INTERGFACES

User initiated borders fall into tow estimated classes:

1. Command pushed boundaries: in this form of interface the consumer inputs guidelines or queries which are taken by means of the pc.

2 The varieties involved with interface is chosen when you consider that it is the first-rate optimum.

COMPUTER-INITIATED INTERFACES

The next laptop – initiated interfaces have been used:

1.The menu process for the consumer is presented with a list of possible choices and the user chooses one; of choices.

2. Questions – reply kind dialog approach the place the pc asks question and takes action established on the basis of the customers reply.

Correct from the start the process goes to be menu driven, the hole menu shows the on hand choices. Deciding on one choice offers one other popup menu with extra choices. In this approach every option leads the customers to data entry form where the user can key in the data.

ERROR MESSAGE DESIGN:

The design of error messages is an vital part of the user interface design. As user is bound to commit some errors or other while designing a system the system should be calculated to be supportive by so long as the user with information

3.3 Planning Scheduling

PLANNING: -

Planning may also be though as selecting all the small tasks that have got to be carried out to accomplish the purpose. Planning additionally takes into consideration , principles , often called constraints which is deploy in our challenge when dissimilar tasks can or are not able to materialize..

SCHEDULING: -

Education can be notion as influential whether or not enough assets are to be had to hold to the plan. Proper Gantt chart and database analysis studies approaches of the development will be shown in this challenge.

GANTT CHART: -

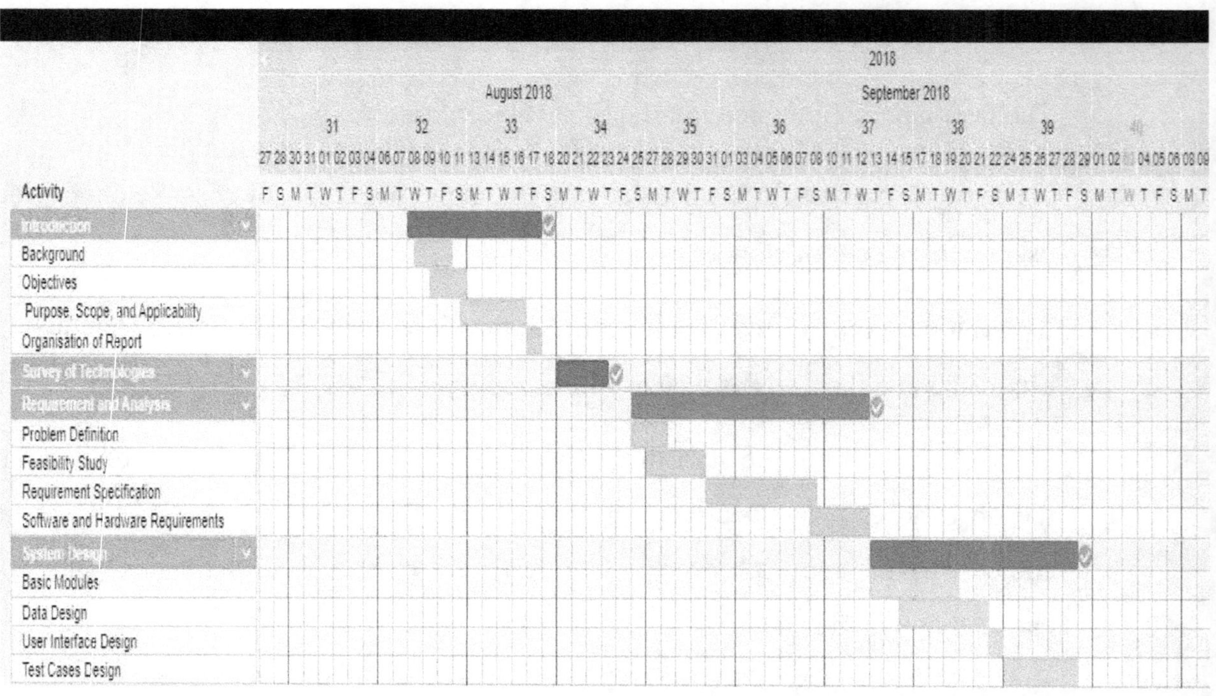

3.4 Software and Hardware Requirements

HARDWARE REQUIREMENTS

I3 Processor based computer

1 GB RAM

50 GB Hard Disk

Monitor

Internet Connection

SOFTWARE REQUIREMENTS

Windows 7 or higher

WAMP server

Notepad++

My SQL 5.1

3.4 Preliminary Product Description

The requirements gather from the source that is the institutes and colleges. Everything is progressing in the computer world, so think about innovative in every field. In the educational field the student evaluation system is the best part in it. This system keeps track of student's marks and attendance. There are three functions that involve in the student evaluation system. Internal marks, external marks and attendance. Fuzzy logic is used to make the system more accurate and successful.

3.5 Conceptual Models

ER DIAGRAM: -

The following are the E-R Diagrams for our system.

3.6.1 E-R diagram for complaints

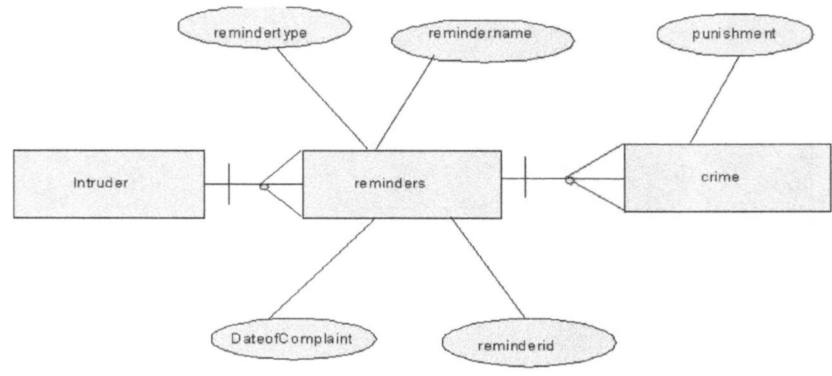

Fig 3.6.2 : E-R diagram for reminders

ACTIVITY DIAGRAM: - ADMIN:

3.6.3 ACTIVITY DIAGRAM:

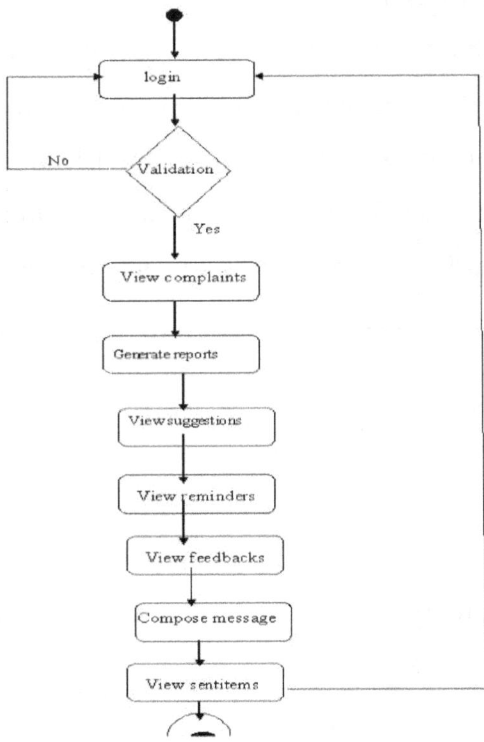

Fig:3.6.3 Activity Diagram for Administrator

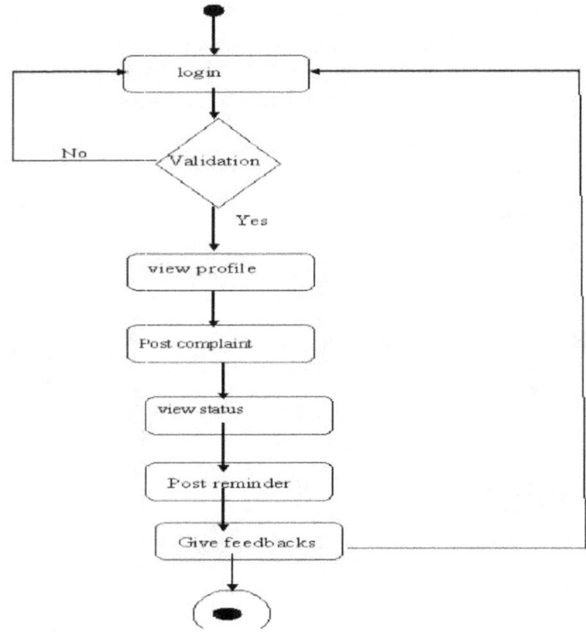

Fig: 3.6.4 Activity Diagram for User

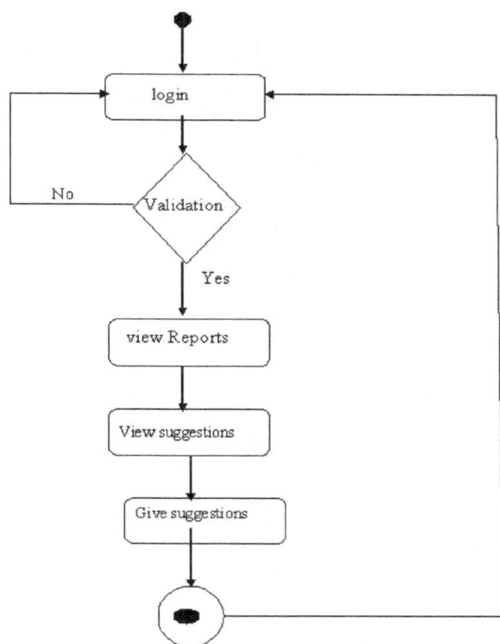

Fig:3.6.5. Activity Diagram for Department

CHAPTER 4: SYSTEM DESIGN

INTRODUCTION

Application design sits on the technical kernel of the application engineering method and is The clothier's purpose is to provide a model or representation of an entity to be able to later be developed. Opening, once systemconditionhave been exact and analyzed, procedure design is the first of the three technical movements -design, code and experiment that is required to construct and affirm utility. .

The value will also be recounted with a single word "excellent". Design is the one way that we can effectively translate a customer's view right into a completed software product or process. Software design serves as a groundwork for the entire application engineering steps that comply with. With out a robust design we threat constructing an unstable method – one on the way to be complicated to scan, one whose fine are not able to be assessed except.

For the duration of design, innovative refinement of information structure, software constitution, and procedural details are developed reviewed and documented. System design may also be seen from both technical or task administration point of view. From the technical factor of view, design is made out of 4 events – architectural design, data constitution design, interface design and procedural design.

4.1 Basic Models

Here the overall system will be divided into small modules and ready to be executed one by one. These modules will be further implemented together to make a whole project. The main objective to divide the overall components into small modules is to each part and develops each part or module separately. After successful development of each module we will/can integrate all the modules into one system.

Some important modules that are divided from the system to develop it separately are: -

DATA DICTIONARY:

Table Name: Registration

Sno	Column Name	Data type	Description	Remarks
1.	typeofuser	Varchar	typeofuser	Primary key
2.	usernamae	Varchar	username	Not null
3.	password	Varchar	password	Not null
4.	Phoneno	Number	Phone number	Not null
5.	email	Varchar	Email	Not null
6	question	Varchar	question	Not null
7	answer	Varchar	answer	Not null

Table 3.2.Registation Database

Table Name: Compliant

sno	Column Name	Data type	Description	Remarks
1	complaint no	int	complaint no	Primary key
2	complaintername	Varchar	complaintername	Not null
3	to mail	Varchar	tomail	Not null
4	from mail	varchar	From mail	Not null
5	subject	varchar	subject	Not null
6	description	varchar	subject	Not null
5	time	varchar	subject	Not null

Table 3.3 complaint Database

Table Name: thieve information

Sno	Column Name	Data type	Description	Remarks
1	thievename	varchar	thievename	Primary key
2	noofcrime	Varchar	noofcrime	Not null
3	indentity	image	indentity	Not null
2	reward	Varchar	reward	Not null

4.2 Data Design

4.2.1 schema design

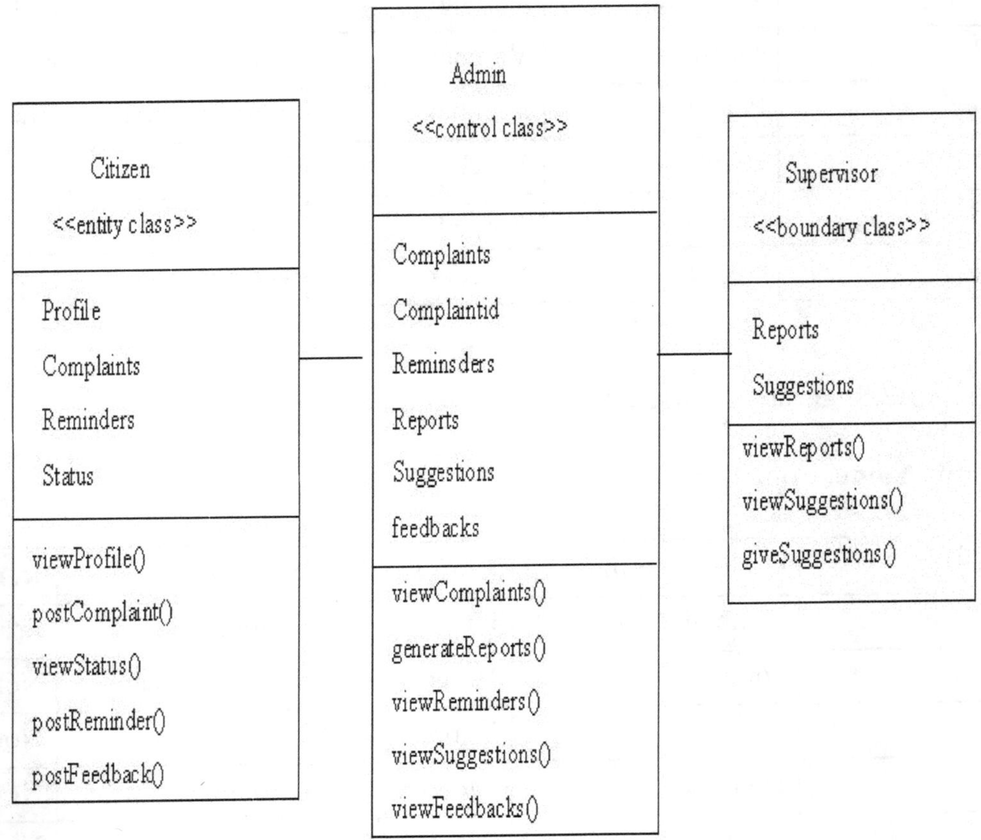

CLASS DIAGRAM

4.2.2 DATA INTEGRITY AND CONSTRAINTS

Data integrity and constraints are important because we are using MYSQL data base. So shows how a key is dependent and independent on each other. In student evaluation system if there are a risk in the database the integrity constraints is used to guard against accidental damage. Insertion, updating and deletion done carefully because this operation should affect the data integrity.

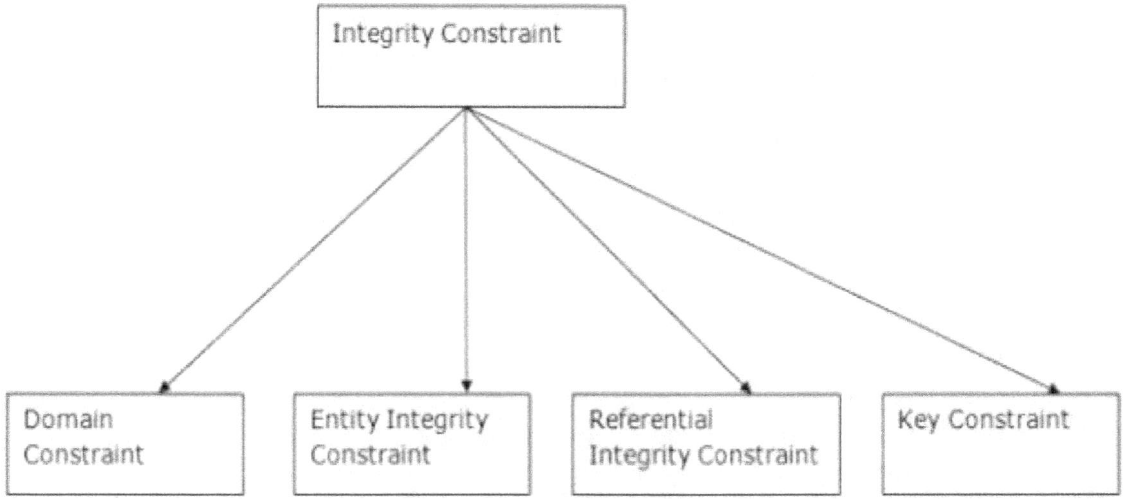

4.3 Procedural Design

4.3.1 LOGIC DIAGRAM

DATA FLOW

1) an info glide has only one direction of go with the run between symbols. It may float in both recommendations between a procedure and an information retailer to exhibit a learn earlier than an update. The later is by and large indicated nevertheless with the aid of two separate arrows since these happen at unique variety.

2) A become a member of in DFD means that precisely the same information comes from any of two or more exclusive approaches information store or sink to a original area.

3) a knowledge float can not go directly again to the same method it leads. There ought to be atleast one other system that handles the data waft produce some other data waft returns the original data into the commencing approach.

4) a data go with the flow to a data store means replace (delete or exchange).

5) a knowledge float from a data retailer approach retrieve or use.

An know-how float has a noun phrase label a couple of knowledge glide noun phrase can exhibit up on a single arrow provided that the complete flows on the same arrow switch mutually as one bundle.

4.3.2 Data structure

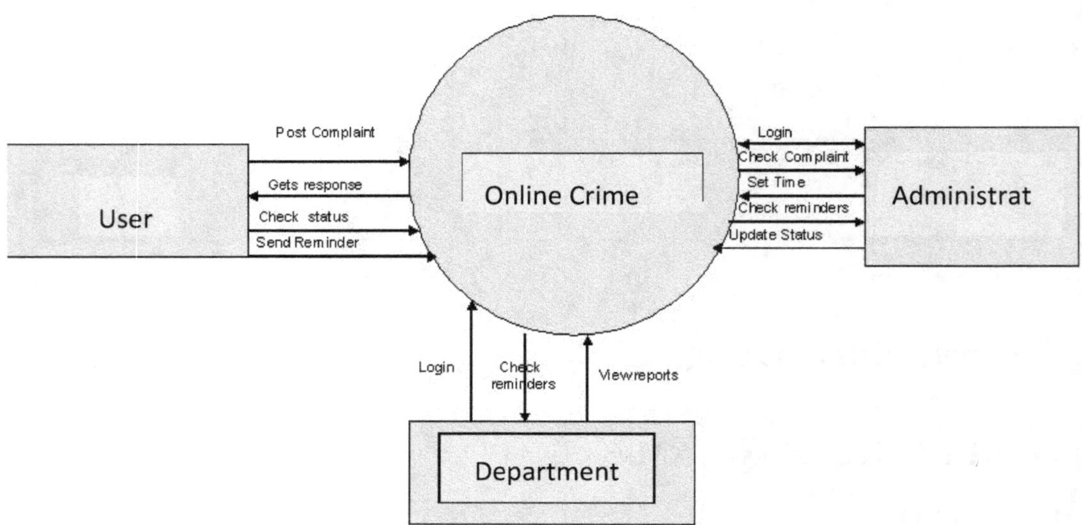

Fig 4.3.1 Context free Dig. for Online crime System

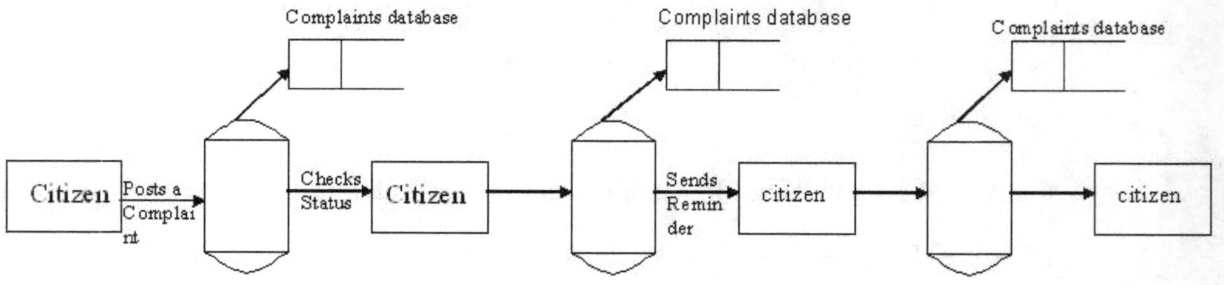

Fig 4.3.2 level1 for user

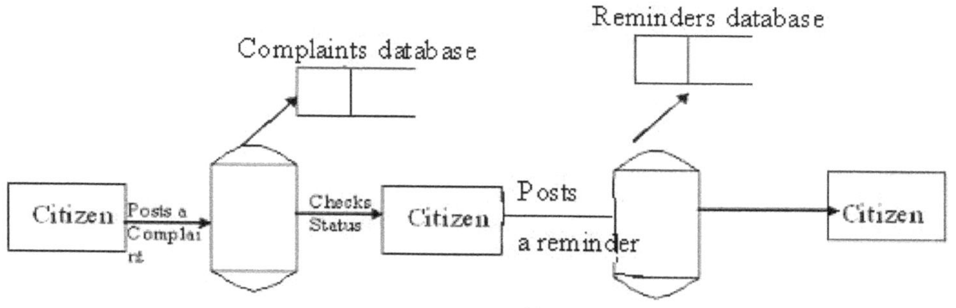

Fig 4. 3.3 level 2 for user

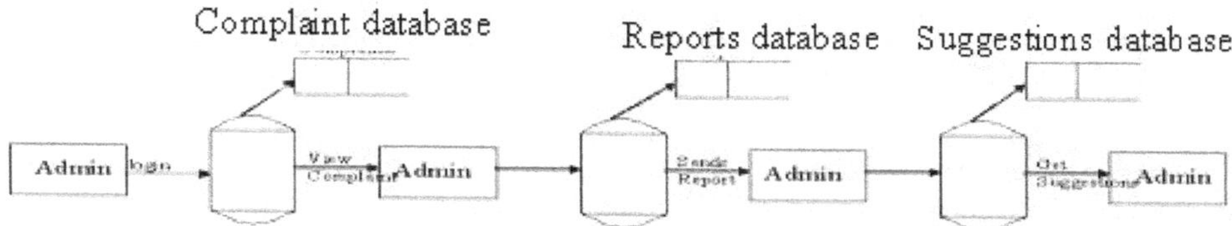

Fig4:4.3.4 level 1 diag for Commissioner

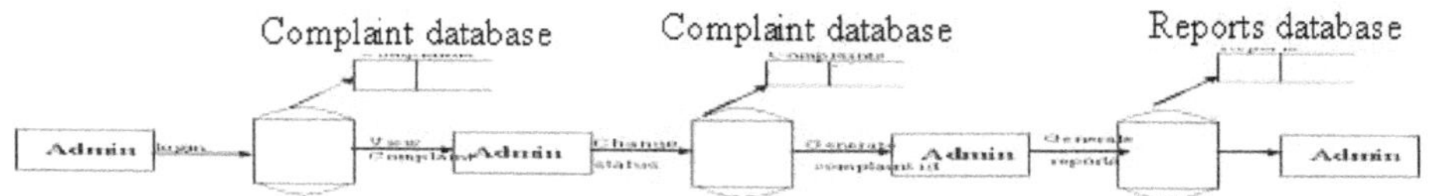

Fig :4.3.5 leve2 Diag. for Commissioner

Fig:4.3.6 level1 diagram for Department

4.3.3 Algorithem design:

Algorithm for User

Step 1: Open the Web Site

Step 2: Login the web site as User

Step 3:Check for the valid login

And if not valid then go to Step-2

else go to Step-4

Step 4: Edit Design

Step 5: Manage Images

Step 6: Manage pages

Step 7: Manage Extras

Step 8: Messages

Step 9: Personal Preference

Step 10: Exit

Algorithm for Manage Pages

Step 1:If you select the page list or Add page.

Step 2:If you select the Add page and click on submit button.

Else you select the page list you will provide 2 option.

Step 3: if you are select the 1st option i.e. edit page than you click on submit button and save on it.

Else you select 2nd option i.e. delete page the pop window shown and ask you are you sure to delete the pages.

Step 4: If you select yes than your pages has deleted successfully.

Else it goes step-2.

Step 5:exit.

4.4 User Interface

LOGIN PAGE:

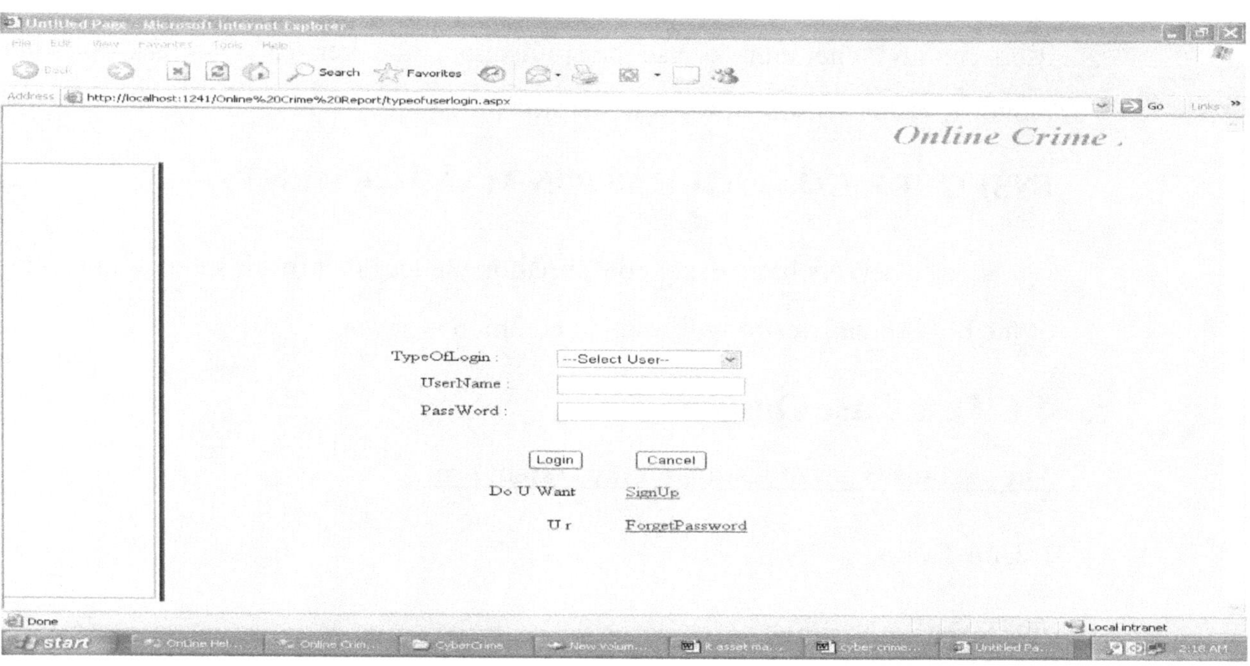

4.5 Security Issues

NON-VALIDATED INPUT: -

Attackers can use information not confirmed before used by our tender to reach backend components.

INJECTION FLAWS: -

purposes move limits when it accesses external approach or the neighborhood OS. If an attacker embeds malicious commands within the parameters, the outside approach could execute these commands on behalf of the appliance.

IMPROPER ERROR HANDLING: -

Refers to error stipulations that arise for the period of usual operations that aren't handled properly. Attackers can use these to obtain special system knowledge, deny carrier, and motive security mechanisms to fail or crash the server.

DENIAL OF SERVICE: -

Attackers can eat our software assets on the factor where different respectable users can no longer entry or use the application. Attackers can also lock users out of their money owed or reason an software to fail.

INSECURE CONFIGURATION MANAGEMENT: -

web servers have many conformation choices that result safety and aren't easy out of the box. Having a strong formation common is severe.

4.6 Test Case Design

The various types of testing on the system are:

1. Unit Testing.

2. Integration Testing

3. System testing

4. User Acceptance Testing

1.Unit Testing:

Unit testing centers endeavors around the littlest unit of programming outline. This is otherwise called module testing. The modules are tried independently. The test is completed amid programming stage itself. In this progression, every module is observed to work tasteful as respects to the normal yield from the module.

2. Integration Testing:

Information can be lost over an interface. One module can adversy affect another, sub capacities, when consolidated, may not be connected in wanted way in real capacities. Incorporation testing is a deliberate methodology for building the program structure, while in the meantime leading test to reveal blunders related inside the interface. The goal is to take unit tried modules and constructs program structure. Every one of the modules are consolidated and tried in general.

3. Framework Testing:

Framework testing is the phase of usage. This is to check whether the framework works precisely and productively before live activity begins. Testing is crucial to the accomplishment of the framework. The competitor framework is liable to an assortment of tests: on line reaction, volume, push, recuperation, security and convenience tests. A progression of tests are performed for the proposed framework is prepared for client acknowledgment testing.

4. Client Acknowledgment Testing:

Client acknowledgment of a framework is the key factor for the achievement of any framework. The framework under thought is tried for the client acknowledgment by always staying in contact with the planned framework clients at the season of creating and rolling out improvements at whatever point required.

- Validation:

At the zenith of the coordination testing, Programming is totally collected as a bundle. Interfacing mistakes have been revealed and rectified and a last arrangement of programming test start in approval testing. Approval testing can be characterized from various perspectives, yet a basic definition is that the approval succeeds when the product capacities in a way that is normal by the client. After approval test has been led, one of the three conceivable conditions exists.

a)The capacity or execution qualities affirm to determination and are acknowledged.

b)A deviation from particular is revealed and a lack records is made.

c)Proposed framework under thought has been tried by utilizing approval test and observed to work attractive.

- Output Testing:

Subsequent to playing out the approval testing, the following stage is yield trying of the proposed framework, since no framework could be valuable in the event that it doesn't create the required yield in a particular arrangement. The yield organize on the screen is observed to be right, the configuration was planned in the framework configuration time as per the client needs. For the printed copy likewise; the yield comes according to the predefined necessities by the client. Subsequently yield testing did not result in any amendment for the framework.